The Ultim(

Brain Plasticity!

Change Your Brain And Increase Your Brain Power Fast Using These Powerful Brain Training And Brain Change Strategies!

Ryan Cooper

STOP!!! Before you read any further....Would you like to know the Success Secrets of how to make Passive Income Online?

If your answer is yes, then you are not alone. Thousands of people are looking for the secret to learning how to create their own online passive income style business.

If you have been searching for these answers without much luck, you are in the right place!

Because I want to make sure to give you as much value as possible for purchasing this book, right now for a limited time you can get 3 incredible bonuses for free.

At the end of this book I describe all 3 bonuses. You can access them at the end. But for those of you that want to grab your bonuses right now. See below.

Just Go Here For Free Instant Access:

www.OperationAwesomeLife.com/FreeBonuses

Legal Notice

Disclaimer Notice

Table Of Contents

Introduction

I want to thank you and congratulate you for purchasing the book, *"Brain Plasticity: The Ultimate Guide To Brain Plasticity! - Change Your Brain And Increase Your Brain Power Fast Using These Powerful Brain Training And Brain Change Strategies!"*

Brain Plasticity And Wildly Effective Brain Change Strategies That Work For Anyone At Any Age!

This book contains proven steps and strategies on how to understand brain plasticity and how you can quickly and efficiently change your brain to be the most effective and useful to help you reach desired outcomes in your life!

Our brains are so powerful and most people hardly even tap into the almost limitless potential our brains are capable of. People tend to allow life circumstances to dictate where our physical life goes, not knowing that a change in the physical world must first have a change in the mental world.

Brain Plasticity will help you understand through advances in neuroscience just how you can form new neural pathways so your desired outcomes will become reality. If you feel like you aren't getting anywhere in life and you're beginning to think that you're powerless, you need to take advantage of your brain's plasticity.

In other words, you shouldn't waste any more time. If you want to start living your life the way you want to, you need to read this right away and start changing your brain through the fastest means possible.

Thanks again for purchasing this book, I hope you enjoy it!

Chapter 1 - How Brain Plasticity Can Benefit You

The most modern and the latest brain research tell us that the human brain is more pliable and more moldable than originally thought. If you have this notion that the brain is rigid, then you are wrong. In fact, throughout our life, we can shape, grow, and further improve our cognitive abilities and our level of intelligence. What's great about this is that it debunks the notion that we can no longer do anything to compensate for the lost opportunities to develop our intellect when we were younger. We can do a lot to improve our brains no matter what our age may be.

There are two common ways to benefit from this. The first option is to master the mechanism and dynamics of the brain by learning how to fully operate it. The second option is for you to learn new ways to grow the skills that you already possess further. An essential part of this is striking the perfect balance between your EQ (emotional quotient) and IQ (intelligence quotient). An important component of brain plasticity is increasing your level of awareness on how the brain truly works.

In order to fully grasp the concept of brain plasticity, you need to first understand the new view on intelligence. In the modern view devised by Howard Gardner, it was proposed that intelligence comes in different forms. This veers from the conventional view that intelligence can only be gauged by looking at a person's cognitive capabilities. Based on the theory of multiple intelligences, the brain can be considered as an all-in-one and all-purpose machine. It operates independent of context and content.

Howard Gardner, tagged as the father of multiple intelligences, believes that there are eight different types of intelligences. This is a big counterstatement to the usual notion that intelligence can only be measured by looking closely at analytic, verbal, and mathematical skills. Have you noticed that with time, more and more millionaires produced by this society aren't even holders of any college degrees? This is a clear testimonial that school may be good at developing some kinds of intelligence, but not all.

With the mastery of brain plasticity, you will learn how to develop not just your cognitive skills. You will also have the opportunity to mold your other aspects of intelligence. You might be wondering what intelligences could be furthered with the techniques prescribed by brain plasticity. Here are the multiple intelligences according to Howard Gardner:

1. Verbal-linguistic: This refers to a person's capability to use words properly and notice linguistic expressions right away. People like speakers, poets, and teachers have this and they are able to articulate their ideas easily in terms of spoken and written words.
2. Logical-mathematical: This intelligence applies to engineers, accountants, and scientists. It refers to the person's capability to apply the concepts of logic and apply the rules of numbers. This is manifested by the capability to solve scientific and mathematical problems easily. They are "naturals" when they are around numbers. They can easily decipher patterns and relationships.
3. Visual-spatial: People like sculptors, visual artists, architects, and pilots are quite superior in this aspect. They are very much aware of the spatial interrelation of objects. They are also good in visualizing, especially when it comes to perspective. People with superior visual-spatial intelligence can easily do mental manipulation of objects, point out existing patterns, adjust the field of vision, and sense comparative dimensions.
4. Body-kinesthetic: These people are most aware of sensations and movements. They also have great dexterity and above par hand-eye coordination. They are great at physical and fluid control. They remember things by doing and they utilize their muscle memory. The best examples of people who are very intelligent in this aspect are mechanics, athletes, surgeons, and dancers.
5. Interpersonal: Leaders, CEOs, politicians, pastors, and psychologists are usually superior in this aspect. This is the capability to respond and pick up signals that are not uttered through words. They can readily see the world through other people's eyes. They do well in interacting with others. They can read through people's desires, emotions, and motivations.
6. Musical: Conductors, DJs, and songwriters are known for being naturally comfortable and attuned to music, sound,

and rhythm. They also have the ability to accurately detect tunes, voice pitch, and tonality. They can compose music, perform, or simply appreciate the craft.

7. Intrapersonal: They are the ones who have mastered the dynamics of their own thinking and feelings. They can interpret their own attitudes, moods, and physical signals. They are the ones who wish to better understand their own intentions, emotions, desires, and motivations. This is found in people like spiritual leaders, entrepreneurs, and artists.

8. Nature: They are very sensitive of the elements of the natural world. They explore the environment and the creatures that live in it. This is best manifested by geologists, botanists, and biologists.

To reiterate, the brain is like a very young puppy – it can be trained. You just have to "befriend" your own so that you can be comfortable in teaching it some new tricks. There are different techniques that you can use and you can learn more about them in this compendium.

Chapter 2 - Scientific Proof That Brain Plasticity Works At Any Age

As we age, our brain still undergoes growth and development. Among the most startling and surprising revelations in the modern world is that even adults have the opportunity to maximize the potential of their intellect through brain plasticity. There was this old notion wherein it was suggested that only young kids can improve through brain plasticity. But with the most sophisticated technologies at hand, this old notion was proven to be wrong.

Neurogenesis, more popularly known as brain plasticity, refers to the brain's capability to undergo changes *throughout* a human being's life. This happens through the formation of new connections in between each brain cell. This can alter or enhance the brain function. There is scientific proof that the changing and furthering of brain cell connection happens even when a person is in his advanced age.

The bits of evidence were collected based on different kinds of observations. For example, in a study conducted among cab drivers in London, scientists have discovered that they underwent a greater degree of brain plasticity compared to bus drivers. Later on, the phenomenon was explained by the fact that bus drivers have a fixed route followed. On the other hand, an average cab driver in London has to be familiar with 25 thousand streets. The part of their brain that has something to do with map reading and navigation grew, and this is true across different ages. This only goes to show that the brain possesses an active mechanism for neurological growth – as opposed to the old belief that it only housed millions of brain cells while they are waiting for their death.

Also, plasticity was observed among people who are capable of speaking another language aside from their mother tongue. It seems like that second language acquisition can only be possible through some significant changes that happen in the internal structure of the brain. This is located at the very back part of the cell mass. Usually, those who have more than one language have enlarged back parts (specifically the left side) of the brain.

Differences were also noted in the brains of people who are inclined to doing music as compared to those who don't. The volume of the brain of musicians is found to be highest among professionals. On the other hand, those who do not do music at all have the lowest brain volume.

Also, an extensive degree of learning that is abstract in nature can lead to some significant changes in the brain. In another study, the brains of students were examined before and after an exam (three months in between). Their brains were found to undergo changes in the regions that are involved in learning and memory retrieval. This did not happen to the brains of the control group – those who did not study or prepare for an exam. No change was noted in the brains of those who did not study for an exam.

These bits of evidence only popularize the idea that the adult brain is more malleable than we all think it is. The brain, therefore, regenerates throughout a person's life. In the same way, deterioration in the brain can happen if a person does not do anything to improve his level of intelligence. If you wish to maintain or further improve the state of your brain, you need to do mental and physical exercises. It is also important to expose yourself to activities for environmental enrichment.

So, if you are already an adult, it is not yet too late to hone your capabilities by altering your brain functions. There are many computer programs that can definitely help you in effectively accomplishing this. There are other suggestions that you may try: begin writing using your non-dominant hand, learn a new language, listen to different songs of birds and attempt to identify what kind of birds they are, learn playing a new instrument, and master some new mathematics skills.

Chapter 3 - Understanding Brain Plasticity And How It Actually Works

Brain plasticity is also referred to as cortical remapping or neuroplasticity. It refers to the ability of the brain to undergo change and to adapt itself to the experiences that the individual undergoes. Until the 1960s, experts believed that the brain can only undergo changes during the period of infancy and childhood. But as established in the previous chapter of this compendium, it is quite clear that even adults can still hone their mental and intellectual capabilities via brain plasticity.

Brain Plasticity History

It was William James, a psychologist, who was fist to give the suggestion that the brain undergoes changes as opposed to the popular belief. This suggestion was made as early as the 1890s. He wrote that the nerves and the brain tissues, as he suspects, are likely to be given the capacity to be of acceptable level of plasticity. For many years, this suggestion was ignored and even actively opposed by other "experts" in the field.

In the 1920s, it was Karl Lashley who was first to provide research-based and scientific evidence that, indeed, changes occur in the brain, as manifested by rhesus monkeys. Four decades after, there were researchers who started looking into the cases of adults (in much more advanced ages) who have suffered from stroke and have regained their functioning. This is another manifestation on how moldable the brain can be.

These are just some researches that show how the brain can be made to undergo change and rewire itself to cope with the stimuli presented by the environment.

So, how does the concept of brain plasticity work exactly?

All in all, the human brain consists of almost 100 billion nerve cells. The old concept is that right after birth, neurogenesis (or the creation of new nerve cells) stops. This has been debunked because there are supporting studies that tell us that the brain is truly capable of creating new neurons and establishing new connections between nerve cells.

The following are the key information that you need to know about brain plasticity or neuroplasticity:

- Plasticity can vary by age. It can happen throughout your lifetime. There are specific kinds of changes that are dominant for certain life stages.
- Brain plasticity involves many different processes. It is continuous and it occurs from the beginning until the end of life. Aside from neurons, it also involves vascular cells and glial cells.
- Brain plasticity can happen because of any of the following: as a result of brain damage or as a consequence of learning, memory formation, and experience.
- Environmental factors in the process of brain plasticity. In addition, genetics is also a determinant.

The first years of human life are crucial because the growth of the brain is rapid. Right after birth, the neurons located at the cerebral cortex can be estimated to have 2,500 synapses. Three years after, the number of synapses would increase six folds (up to 15,000 synapses).

Adults, on the average only have around 7,500 to 8,000 synapses. Why is there a decrease? Neurologists explain that this is due to synaptic pruning. As we age, there are connections that are strengthened, and there are others that are eliminated. Those that are frequently used tend to be stronger. Those connections that aren't used are eventually eliminated.

What are the two types of brain plasticity?

Based on research, there are two types of brain plasticity: functional plasticity and structural plasticity. Functional plasticity pertains to the ability of the brain to move its functions, from parts of the brain that are damaged to parts of the brain that are not damaged. On the other hand, structural plasticity pertains to the capability to make structural change as a result of experience and learning.

Chapter 4 - The Easiest And Most Effective Brain Plasticity Techniques

Again, brain plasticity is your brain's innate capacity to undergo changes – be it chemical, functional, or physical – throughout your life. Plasticity is also the major basis for brain training techniques and exercises.

Treatments that are Non-Invasive

The easiest and the most effective brain plasticity technique are those that are non-invasive and those that do not involve any drugs. Most of them rely on an intensive training process that dwells on challenging activities and repetitions. This is said to be one of the most exciting ways because it is self-paced and the results are usually very satisfactory.

Revolutions on Plasticity

Brain health and science is on the verge of revolution because of the growing knowledge about plasticity. There are luminaries, scientists, and institutions around the world that are looking at therapies as a means not just to improve oneself but also to address several cognitive problems. The programs on brain plasticity are actually based on the programs that might help those with cognitive problems in their respective attempts to lead a normal life. On the other hand, there are artists who experience conditions, like focal dystonia, that use brain plasticity techniques so that they can go back to playing music again. Additionally, there are cancer patients who use brain plasticity to be able to do their old roles again. For those with Alzheimer's disease, brain plasticity techniques and exercises are used to put a stop to the progression of their condition. And yes, there are many people who just want to learn new things and improve in their respective fields.

Brain Plasticity Daily Exercise

These exercises are actually designed to improve the function of the brain. You can do these even without the assistance of a professional neurologist. There is a wide array of choices; however, you should always look into their scientific bases before trying them out. Those with established scientific guidelines are likely to be more effective.

How will you classify neuroplasticity techniques?

The neuroplasticity programs hone the inherent plasticity of the brain. The remodeling process goes on throughout one's life. With exercise and training, you can give direction to your progress.

Chapter 5 - Neuro Linguistic Programming And Brain Plasticity

Brain plasticity is also defined as the capability of the brain to undergo change – be it for the better or for the worse all throughout your life. Therefore, the brain is far from being static. It is not fixed. On the contrary, it is adaptable and dynamic.

But you need to understand that brain plasticity is more of a physical type of process. Literally, the brain's gray matter can either thicken or shrink. The pathways of the neurons can be improved or developed. In the same way, it can become disconnected or weakened. Positive changes usually result to a newly acquired skill. Negative changes usually result to forgetting a fact or losing a skill.

With the dawn of a new research era, brain plasticity has reached a new height when it comes to brain science and brain health. The implications are truly far reaching. All over the world, scientists are devising new therapies linked to neuro linguistic programming and brain plasticity. Therefore, it goes beyond the mechanisms of the brain. Instead, it tends to cover other relevant areas and fields of study.

In recent efforts, brain plasticity principles were applied in order to help out patients who are trying to recover from fibromyalgia, ME/CFS, and other diseases related to this. Most of the research efforts are actually centered on the amygdala. The amygdala is an almond-shaped structure that has a connection to the nervous system. In the brain, there are two amygdalae, one on each side.

You might be wondering what the role of amygdala is. Primarily, it helps in protecting a person from danger. It is tasked in interpreting stimuli to tell if danger is coming. It works in close coordination with the hypothalamus to choose between two programmed reactions: fight or flight.

For example, in the case of ME/CFS, the amygdala seems not to be able to do its job properly. The stimulation is very minimal and it gets stuck in the state of high level of alertness. Therefore, even after the danger, the body will be programmed to feel heightened fear and other emotions. This can be very harmful for the body because it can have adverse effects to both endocrine and immune systems. It leads to a wide range of symptoms.

Therapists, analysts, and researchers say that the programming and retraining technique for amygdala is actually based on the process of brain plasticity. It was hypothesized that the recovery from this particular condition needs to involve new neural pathways that will connect the amygdala and the medial prefrontal cortex. The medial prefrontal cortex is capable of controlling the level of sensitivity of the amygdala. That way, it will be able to safely and effectively monitor threat. In addition, it will be programmed to regulate responses of the emotion, like fear.

The retraining and programming of the amygdala employs mind power to heal all the parts of the body. Further techniques are derived from Neuro Linguistic Programming, breathing methods, meditation, and visualization.

The brain training programs usually yield the most beneficial of results. Though it may be difficult to truly understand the mechanism of brain plasticity, it is something that has been proven and supported by scientific evidence.

Chapter 6 - Advanced Autosuggestion And Brain Plasticity

The law of attraction simply states that "you will get what you want badly." If there is a genuine feeling of affinity to success and it becomes a fixture of the mind, then there is a high chance of turning that desire into a reality. This is the very foundation of the principle of autosuggestion. Because of the fact that if you put your focus on something, by virtue of autosuggestion, you will be able to decipher ways to develop these desires, intents, dreams, and hopes into reality.

When a person becomes fully aware of his dreams, thoughts, and aspirations, he will unconsciously integrate related practices into his lifestyle. In addition, constantly thinking of the things you've long desired can lead to some changes in the structure of the brain and this is in line with the principles of brain plasticity. In the end, you will see that the thoughts that you embed into your mind can be manifested in real life.

By the principles of autosuggestion, when a person effectively generate the specific thoughts that need to be conceived, he should first know and fully realize what he wants in his life. Truth be told, the brain is analogous to a personal computer. It is meant to provide results based on the specific directions or commands that you feed it. Hence, if a person wishes to achieve a certain outcome, he needs to generate brand new directions so that the thoughts will be deeply embedded in a person's lifestyle. By analogy, if the laptop or computer is the brain, the programmers or the software are the specific steps in attaining the goals and desires.

Most of the beliefs that we hold on to are usually anchored to what we have acquired since our childhood. In order to be successful in our lives, we need to use the power of new suggestions within one's mind in order to eventually turn thoughts into reality. The procedure is popularly known as subliminal messaging or autosuggestion.

With time, the farther we go with embedding new suggestions into your mind, the greater chance you have to embed the suggestion into the structure of your brain via brain plasticity. When you proceed quickly with the process of embedding new beliefs in the brain subconsciously, your personal reality will soon synchronize and adjust with the new beliefs that you currently have. Always remember that if you will not choose to shape the reality, the reality will take over and shape who you are. Take over and be in total control.

Chapter 7 - How To Increase Memory Improvement Through Brain Plasticity

Memory, by definition, is concerned with the processes involved in the recording and accessing or retrieval of information about events, people, and places. It is also concerned with the individual's capability to do the encoding, storing, and retrieving of information that was acquired. The process of encoding is the representation of acquired information. The process of storing involves the process of rehearsing the information through repetitive actions. Finally, retrieval refers to the searching of acquired information from materials and information that was previously stored.

The formation of memories in the brain happens as a result of the combination of neural impulses. The neural impulses pave the way to the formation of neural pathways. These are mainly accountable as the main memory reservoir.

Perhaps you have heard of many things about memory improvement. But yes, you can do something to improve your memory – thanks to plasticity. By means of reorganizing the neural pathways, you will find it easier to retain information, learn a new skill and memorize it. Research efforts reveal that the brain remains plastic no matter what your age is. There are brain exercises that can help you with this.

These are just some of the exercises that you may try to improve your memory:

Paying attention to visual cues:

1. You may observe nature, colorful objects, paintings, drawings, hoarding, different sizes, and shapes, or anything that is visually appealing for a pre-decided period of time. Using a timer, you can keep track of the time that you are spending. After the observation process, you can record the details you remember on a piece of paper. After writing everything that you have remembered, you may verify if the things you wrote down are valid.

2. Try to sequence and match different things or objects with varying size, colors, and shapes.
3. Spot the difference between two pictures.

Paying attention to auditory cues:

1. Try listening to a set of instructions and carry them out.
2. Listen to different voices of cartoon characters and identify who's who.
3. Group different sounds – vehicles, animals, and musical instruments.
4. Transcribe an audio file.

Paying attention to olfactory cues:

1. The different smells and tastes of food need to be distinguished.
2. For a limited time of tasting, the ingredients used are to be identified and recorded.
3. The ingredients of a certain dish have to be identified after a limited period of time of smelling.

There are many games that can help you increase the capability of your brain to memorize. You need to take on different challenges. If you would not give sufficient challenge to your brain, it will experience deterioration. The degeneration can be countered effectively by presenting new surprising information to your brain.

Many of the brain games can now be found online! And yes, you may access them for free. Most of these games are crafted after the principles of brain plasticity. According to studies, using these principles of brain plasticity are effective in improving skills in reading comprehension, in sharpening a wide range of skills, and in leveling up one's capability to memorize.

Chapter 8 - Using Meditation For Brain Plasticity

Meditation does not only change the state of mind – it also does physical change in your brain. This acquires more scientific evidence with time. And there are correlation studies that suggest the effects of meditation to the brain plasticity. This chapter will focus on the most important findings.

Important Conclusion #1: Cortical thickness is directly proportional to the meditation experience.

This has been proven by Magnetic Resonance Imaging or MRI. According to research, meditators have thicker cortex and compared to non-meditators. Sensory processing and interception are usually associated with attention and memory.

Important Conclusion #2: Gray matter density of the nervous system (the brain stem) is correlated with long-term meditation.

This is according to a study conducted among those who are involved in long-term meditation. They are grouped according to age and this has been confirmed via Magnetic Resonance Imaging.

Important Conclusion #3: Long-term meditation is found to have underlying anatomical correlation. Long-term meditators are associated with greater volume of gray matter and bigger hippocampal regions.

Long-term meditators were compared with participants chosen via matched control sampling. The main conclusion is that those who do long term meditation have higher volumes of gray matter.

Important Conclusion #4: Practicing mindfulness can lead to an increase in gray matter density.

Participants of the 8-week MBSR or Mindfulness-Based Stress Reduction program are found to have increased volume of gray matter in the area near the hippocampus.

Important Conclusion #5: The white matter changes can be induced by meditation.

This can be tested via DTI or Diffusion Tensor Imaging. This is found to help in enhancing the connection in the areas of the brain. The white matter has a great involvement in the interconnection of many areas of the brain. According to experts, it is the relaxation factor provided by meditation that helps in white matter changes.

Chapter 9 - How To Increase Your Concentration Using Brain Plasticity

At this point, you may think of your brain as a muscle in the body. Well, technically, it is not. Essentially, the two share one important thing – they both get stronger when you do more exercise. Every day, when you do cognitive tasks, you can expect to increase your brain capability.

To boost your capability to concentrate, you can use the following brain plasticity techniques:

Brain Plasticity Technique #1: Try to use the non-dominant hand

Trying to tackle new and unfamiliar tasks can improve the capability of your brain to improve your cognitive skills and it can also increase your level of concentration. You brain power may be better boosted if you will try to use the non-dominant hand. You may try to write using your "other" hand. You can also use it in combing your hair, eating, brushing your teeth, and holding the glass while you drink. You may even try holding and controlling the computer mouse using your non-dominant hand.

By doing so, you will successfully stimulate the communication and interconnection between the brain's two hemispheres. It manifests greatly through your physical attributes. You will be healthier and you will feel better inside and out.

Brain Plasticity Technique #2: Work your brain out

Use it or lose it – try to work your brain whenever possible. Create opportunities for mental exercises. Such mental exercises will keep the brain healthy and fit. Among the activities that you can do include doing playing chess, doing crossword puzzles, memorizing objects, names, and phone numbers.

If possible, memorize passages or poems every day. Try to recite them as well. Enhance your vocabulary by learning a new word. Instead of using a calculator, try to calculate manually.

This will help you increase your concentration by creating new neural passages.

Brain Plasticity Technique #3: Move your fingers to improve your brain functions

There is this notion that Asian children are intellectually superior. Experts say that this may be because of the fact that they use their fingers in a more frequent manner. They use it to move the pieces of the abacus at school and they actively use their fingers that have nerve endings on their tips. The sensations you feel through your fingers actually go directly to your brain and it helps increase brain activity.

In order to take full advantage of this biological feature, you might want to try several activities. For example, you may try knitting, crocheting, and the creation of crafts and different artworks that require manipulation with the use of fingers. A more effective way is to try learning how to play stringed instruments, or even the piano.

Chapter 10 - How To Change Your Brain To Obtain Your Goals

The neuro pathways can be formed using the techniques that are discussed throughout this compendium. This leads to the formation of habits. And these habits can fall under two categories – the good ones and the bad ones. In order to achieve success, you need to align your habits with your goals.

In order to be successful, you need to put in some effort. At first, you there will be some form of resistance. If you have sufficient perseverance, intent, and motivation, your brain will form new neural pathways. All you need is to be 100-percent focused.

Before you decide on what areas to develop, you have to set your goals first – both short term and long term. This will help you decide what new skills to learn and what aspects of your personality to enhance.

Thanks to the gift bestowed upon us by neuroplasticity, you can now successfully replace all the undesirable habits that you have and develop new and healthy ones. Take note that this can happen regardless of your age. Regardless if you are a child or an adult, you can enjoy the benefits of neuroplasticity.

One by one, win the battles of the mind. This way, you will triumph in all aspects of your life and achieve success in any goals that you decide to focus on. The benefits go beyond the mental. You will benefit emotionally and physically, too, in the long run.

Conclusion

Thank you again for purchasing this book on brain plasticity!

I am extremely excited to pass this information along to you, and I am so happy that you now have read and can hopefully implement these strategies going forward.

I hope this book was able to help you understand brain change and how to use it to accomplish your desires.

The next step is to get started using this information and to hopefully live a happier, much more fulfilling life!

Please don't be someone who just reads this information and doesn't apply it, the strategies in this book will only benefit you if you use them!

If you know of anyone else that could benefit from the information presented here please inform them of this book.

Finally, if you enjoyed this book and feel it has added value to your life in any way, please take the time to share your thoughts and post a review on Amazon. It'd be greatly appreciated!

Thank you and good luck!

Preview Of:

The Ultimate Guide To:

<u>Communication Skills!</u>

Improve Self Confidence, Leadership, And Charisma To Persuade And Influence People!

Introduction

I want to thank you and congratulate you for purchasing the book, *"Communication Skills: The Ultimate Guide To Communication Skills! - Improve Self Confidence, Leadership, And Charisma To Persuade And Influence People!"*

This "Communication Skills" book contains proven steps and strategies on how to become a more effective communicator, leader, and listener!

In writing this book I decided I wanted to help people to not only become a fantastic communicator and great leader, but I also think it is equally important to become more self confident and to gain skills to persuade and influence people!

In this book's seven simple chapters, you will learn a lot about practical communication skills that you have to master in order to be the best communicator that you can be.

Thanks again for purchasing this book, I hope you enjoy it!

Chapter 1 - Body Language And Communication Skills

Have you ever found yourself in a situation wherein you do not believe what another person is saying to you? Have you ever found yourself not believing that the person speaking to you has enough credibility to say what he is saying? Perhaps, you have found nodding physically but deep inside, your mind is shouting "No!"

The big difference between what a person says and the way we get their message is determined by the speaker's body language marked by the non-verbal cues and signals that they are using. Once you become more aware of these signals, cues, and signs, you will have an edge when it comes to understanding other people and developing your own communication skills.

Sometimes, we encounter situations wherein the subtle and the not-so-subtle signals affect our overall understanding of a message that has been conveyed. These signals usually consist of facial expressions, body movements, gestures, and the shirts in the body posture. The way a person sits, talks, and walks tell a lot about their message because these are reflections of what's going on inside their heads.

In order to become a better communicator yourself, you need to have a better understanding of the body language. This will help you become more aware with the way you choose to communicate. At the same time, you will learn to read what's on other people's minds. To increase your understanding of what other people are truly saying, you also need to become aware of the signals you are personally sending through your own body language.

Note that there are common signs and signals that you have to be aware of. These usually determine whether the person or the message (or both) are worth believing. The following are some of the things that you have to look out for whenever you communicate (note that the "communicator" can be yourself or other people):

1. The communicator's posture: A credible person usually stands tall. His shoulders are always leaning towards the back to avoid curved impression.

2. The communicator's eye contact: This tells a lot about the communicator's sincerity. A communicator who has a good intent usually is confident of looking in the other party's eye. Eye contact usually greatly complements a smiling face.

3. The communicator's gestures with his arms and hands: A good and credible communicator moves his arms and hands in a purposeful and deliberate manner.

4. The communicator's speech: A good communicator never leaves anything to doubt. Usually, a confident communicator delivers his speech clearly and slowly.

5. Tone of the voice: A good communicator keeps the tone of his voice as low as possible. The lower the tone, the more confident and more serious he seems.

Aside from decoding other peoples' body language and signals, an understanding of these elements are truly useful in effectively communicating what you have to say to other people. The knowledge of body language will help you send emotions, feelings, and intent that you want your audience to see. This way, you can create a better impression.

For instance, when you are about to enter a communication situation, of course you want to appear that you are a person of sufficient authority on the subject matter. Of course, you also want to show everyone how confident you are of what you are about to say. By controlling your gestures, posture, tone of voice, among others, you can send all the "confidence signals" despite the fact that deep inside, butterflies are flying in your stomach.

Body language has a great impact in the way you deal with others and in the manner you choose to communicate. They are taken to reflect what's happening deep inside your mind, body, and emotion.

Aside from those mentioned earlier, body language includes leg movements, muscle tension, skin coloring (for example, becoming white faced or flushed red), perspiration rate, and the rate of breathing.

These signals may also vary across cultures. Different nations have different kinds of norms and traditions that have to be carefully accounted for. When you try to get to know a person, these should be included in what you are asking and verifying.

Thanks for Previewing My Exciting Book Entitled:

"Communication Skills: The Ultimate Guide To: Improve Self Confidence, Leadership, And Charisma To Persuade And Influence People!"

To purchase this book, simply go to the Amazon Kindle store and simply search:

"BRAIN PLASTICITY"

Then just scroll down until you see my book. You will know it is mine because you will see my name "Ryan Cooper" underneath the title.

Alternatively, you can visit my author page on Amazon to see this book and other work I have done. Thanks so much, and please don't forget your free bonuses

DON'T LEAVE YET! - CHECK OUT YOUR FREE BONUSES BELOW!

Free Bonus Offer 1: Get Free Access To The OperationAwesomeLife.com VIP Newsletter!

Free Bonus Offer 2: Get A Free Download Of My Friends Amazing Book "Passive Income" First Chapter!

Free Bonus Offer 3: Get A Free Email Series On Making Money Online When You Join Newsletter!

GET ALL 3 FREE

Once you enter your email address you will immediately get free access to this awesome **VIP NEWSLETTER**!

For a limited time, if you join for free right now, you will also get free access to the first chapter of the awesome book "**PASSIVE INCOME**"!

And, last but definitely not least, if you join the newsletter right now, you also will get a free 10 part email series on **10 SUCCESS SECRETS OF MAKING MONEY ONLINE**!

To claim all 3 of your FREE BONUSES just click below!

Just Go Here for all 3 VIP bonuses!

OperationAwesomeLife.com